BASTARDS

ILLEGITIMACY ARCHITECTURE OF POWER

CATERINA MONDRAGON

Bastards: Illegitimacy – Architecture of Power

ISBN: 978-1-9194919-1-2 (Paperback}

ISBN: 978-1-9194919-2-9 {Hardcover}

ISBN: 978-1-9194919-0-5 {eBook}

Cover and interior design by: MV

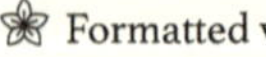 Formatted with Vellum

DEDICATION

To my fellow bastards

those born into questions,

those who entered life without protection or permission,

those who learned to build themselves from the outside in.

May you never again fold yourselves to fit spaces

that were never meant to hold you.

Your beginning was never your boundary.

To the world

may you learn to be kinder next time.

Kinder to the unclaimed, the unnamed, the unprotected.

Kinder to the children whose origins were not their choice,

but whose futures hold more light than their stories suggest.

And to you my MV

legitimate by birth yet Illegitimatised by the world.

Though your path was the opposite of mine,

you walked beside me through every page,

holding the pieces of me that history tried to scatter.

You are art in human form singular, impossible to replace,

unlike anyone I have ever known.

Your mind, your hands, your spirit create beauty in ways the world has no language for.

I love you beyond measure, beyond circumstance,

beyond the boundaries that shaped us both.

You are the one who steadies me,

the one who fixes what breaks,

the one whose quiet strength carries the spine of this book

and the spine of my life.

Without you, none of this would exist.

Not the woman I became while writing them.

CONTENTS

PROLOGUE

No child asks to be born. That fact alone should have made the idea of the bastard impossible.

Instead, societies built entire systems around it.

For centuries, a child's worth was measured not by their existence, but by the circumstances of it. Not by who they were, but by how they arrived. Marriage became the gatekeeper of dignity. Religion became the witness. Law became the enforcer. And the child, silent, blameless, present, became the one to bear the consequence.

The word bastard was never created to describe a child. It was created to protect adults.

It protected inheritance. It protected bloodlines. It protected reputations.

Marriage, as enforced for most of history, was not a romantic institution. It was an economic one, designed to ensure property, power, and legitimacy moved cleanly from one sanctioned generation to the next. Children born inside that structure were secured. Children born outside it were exposed. And so a sentence was passed. Not on those who chose.

Not on those who desired. Not on those who acted. But on the child. A child born outside marriage did not break a rule. Did not betray a vow. Did not offend a God. Yet it was the child who was named, marked, diminished.

If illegitimacy exists at all, it belongs to parents and institutions, not to children. To adults who made decisions. To churches and states that decided those decisions required punishment. To societies that confused order with morality, and lineage with virtue.

Still, the punishment fell downward.

Names withheld. Inheritance denied. Protection withdrawn. Belonging made conditional.

Children were turned into secondary citizens not because they lacked value, but because acknowledging their value threatened the structures that depended on exclusion. And yet, however it came about, being illegitimate is not something to be ashamed of. It is proof of existence. Of survival. Of the simple, defiant fact that, despite circumstance, you were born.

At least one person chose that outcome. Chose consequence over compliance. Chose life over erasure. That is not disgrace. That is origin.

There are things a bastard learns early:

That the world is not fair.

That approval can be revoked without warning.

That belonging is often provisional.

This knowledge changes you.

Many illegitimate children grow up with a heightened awareness of power, how it moves, how it disguises itself as morality, how easily it withdraws protection. They learn to read rooms. To anticipate judgment. To navigate systems that were never designed with them in mind. They grow independent sooner. Suspicious of authority. Less reliant on permission.

Denied inheritance, they learn to create. Denied protection, they learn to endure. Denied legitimacy, they learn to define themselves.

This book is about taking power.

It is about showing, without apology, that people branded as bastards have ruled countries, built empires, reshaped culture, created wealth, and altered the course of history. Not in spite of their exclusion, but often because of it.

It is a challenge to society:

A challenge to the lazy assumption that legitimacy equals worth.

A challenge to the belief that "legitimate" children are inherently superior, safer, or more deserving.

A challenge to institutions that praise order while quietly relying on the innovation of outsiders.

And it is a challenge to bastards themselves.

To those who were made to feel accidental.

To those who sensed their place was conditional.

To those who internalised the idea that they should be grateful merely to exist.

This book offers no consolation.

It offers a demand.

To rise above the sentence.

To refuse the inheritance of shame.

To prove, through presence, contribution, and refusal to shrink, that accident or not, you are meant to be here.

You are meant to occupy your space.

You are meant to take up room.

You are meant to leave a mark.

History shows this with brutal consistency:

Bastards do not wait to be invited.

They do not ask to belong. They build. They endure.

They outgrow the systems that tried to contain them.

The chapters that follow are not exceptions.

They are the record of a sentence that failed.

The shame was never on the child.

It belonged, and still belongs, to the world that underestimated them.

AUTHOR'S NOTE ON LANGUAGE

ON THE WORD "BASTARD"

There is a reason this book uses the word bastard without apology.

For centuries, the term was not an insult but a sentence , a legal and religious designation invented to control inheritance, manage scandal, and protect institutions. It punished children for the decisions of adults. It turned birth into hierarchy, and hierarchy into morality. It justified exclusion, silence, and shame.

The word did the damage. Not the child. This book refuses to pretend otherwise.

It does not replace bastard with gentler terms like "born out of wedlock," "illegitimate," or "non-marital child." Those words are not kinder; they are simply less honest. They conceal the severity of a category designed to diminish human worth.

To reclaim a word, you must speak it plainly.

The individuals in these pages were called bastards, by law, by society, by custom, or by implication. The word shaped their lives, their opportunities, their dangers, and their strategies. To erase the word now would be to erase the reality they lived through.

But this is not a book about reclaiming a slur. It is a book about reversing the direction of its power. Here, bastard does not mean shame. It means refusal. Refusal to accept the place assigned.

Refusal to apologise for origin. Refusal to shrink under judgement.

You may flinch at the word. That is understandable. The discomfort belongs to history, not to the child who bore it.

I use the word bastard because it tells the truth. I use it because it names a system, not a person. I use it because avoiding the word protects the structures that invented it. And because speaking it clearly begins the work of dismantling them.

If the word offends, let the offence remain where it belongs, with the world that created it, not the people who survived it.

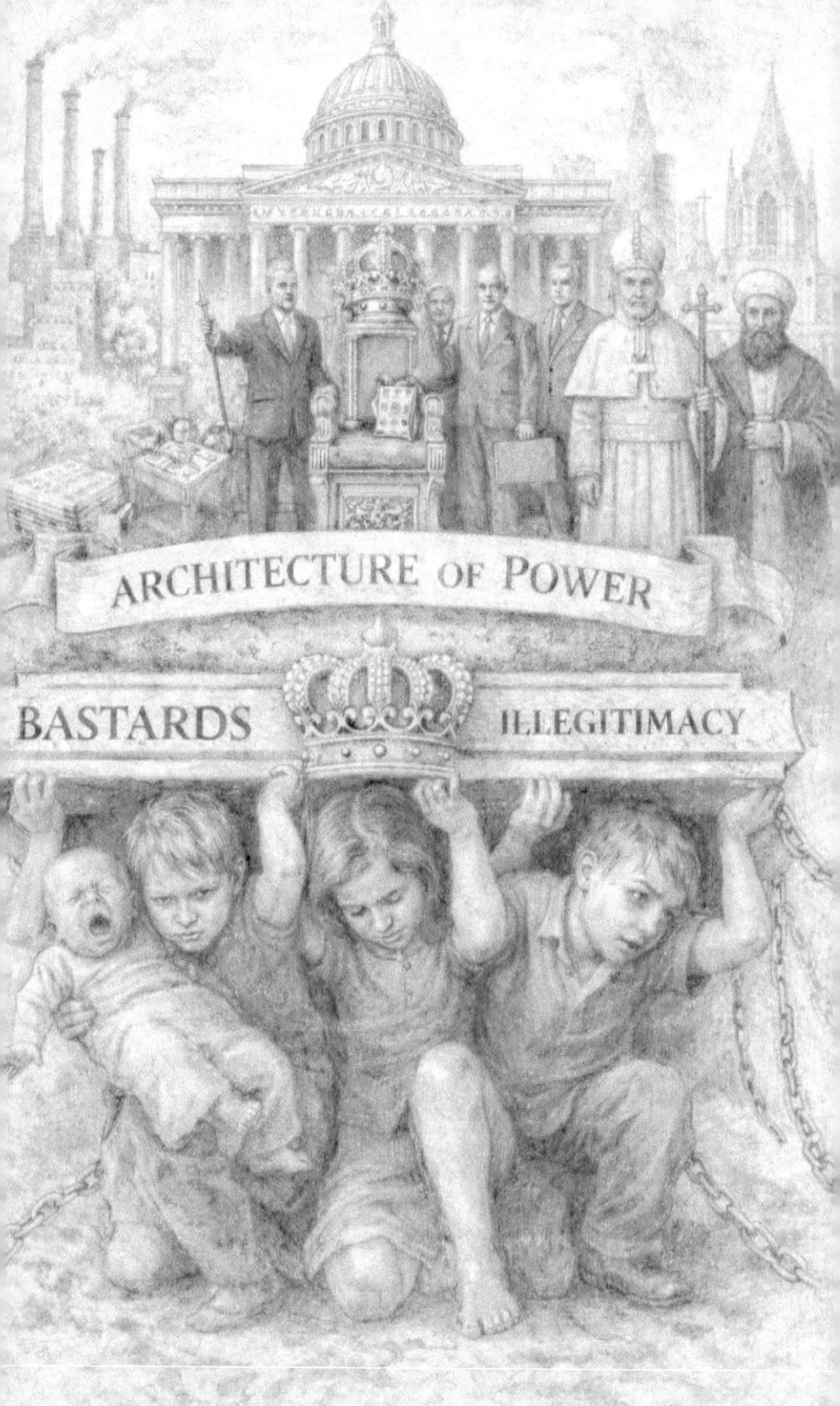
ARCHITECTURE OF POWER
BASTARDS
ILLEGITIMACY

INTRODUCTION

ILLEGITIMACY AS A SOCIAL SENTENCE

This introduction traces how societies created the category of the *bastard*, a legal, religious, and cultural invention designed to control inheritance, preserve power, and discipline desire. It exposes the moral failure of treating birth as destiny, and reveals how the systems meant to diminish illegitimate children instead produced clarity, resilience, and an unusually sharp instinct for survival.

It examines the psychology of those raised without automatic belonging, and how the pressure of exclusion formed minds capable of conquering, creating, and redefining the world.

Above all, it challenges the hierarchies of birth, religion, and legitimacy that still shape modern judgments of worth, asking why a child should ever bear the weight of decisions they did not make, and why society continues to call the innocent illegitimate while excusing the structures that condemned them.

PART I

KINGS WITHOUT CROWNS

INTERLUDE PART I

THE MECHANICS OF SHAME

Shame does not arrive fully formed. It is taught.

Not through direct accusation, children are rarely confronted outright—but through quieter methods: withheld language, altered tone, evasive answers, sudden silences. The illegitimate child learns early that something unspoken surrounds their existence. They feel it long before they understand it.

Shame moves differently from law. Law declares. Shame implies. A child overhears a phrase not meant for them. A relative hesitates before introducing them. A parent answers a question too quickly, or not at all. A teacher glances at a form and pauses just slightly too long.

No one explains the discrepancy between the truth the child lives and the truth adults refuse to name. The silence becomes the lesson. It teaches the child to monitor themselves, to observe before speaking, to anticipate disapproval before it comes. Silence becomes discipline. It requires no enforcer.

This is the invisible labour of the illegitimate mind: to manage the emotions, expectations, and discomforts of others from an age too young to name what they are managing. The legitimate child grows into the world.

The bastard child grows *around* it, navigating gaps, making adjustments, learning when to disappear and when to harden.

Shame, once internalised, becomes self-policing. The child begins to edit their own story to avoid the moment of revelation. They learn which questions are safe, which people can be trusted, which explanations will provoke the frown, the pause, the sudden shift in tone.

This is how the sentence survives even when the law changes.

Legal illegitimacy may be abolished, but social illegitimacy endures in hesitation, in stigma, in inherited patterns of secrecy. The architecture remains, even when the doorways appear open.

Children raised outside permission often grow into adults who anticipate rejection before it arrives. They become hyper-competent or hyper-invisible. They overachieve to outrun implication, or they withdraw to avoid exposure. Some become fiercely independent; others become experts at belonging everywhere except where they were born.

This interlude exists for one reason: to make clear that the damage was not in the word *bastard* alone, but in the systems of silence that shaped the child long before they had language to defend themselves.

Shame survives because it was never merely taught. It was absorbed. This book is not a reconciliation with shame. It is a refusal.

CHAPTER 1

WILLIAM THE BASTARD

ILLEGITIMATE BY BIRTH, LEGITIMATE BY CONQUEST

William was born into power, and denied it at the same time. He came into the world around 1028, the son of Robert I, Duke of Normandy, and Herleva, a woman of no noble standing. Their relationship was not sanctified by marriage.

That single fact would define William's childhood more than blood ever could.

From the moment he could be named, he was marked. *William the Bastard*. It was not a nickname. It was a verdict.

In a world governed by inheritance and legitimacy, William's birth placed him on unstable ground. He had a father with a title, land, and authority, but none of it was securely his. His claim would always be contested. His position would always be conditional. His safety would never be guaranteed.

When William was still a child, his father died suddenly while returning from pilgrimage. Against expectation, and against advice — Robert named his illegitimate son as his heir.

It was an extraordinary decision. And a dangerous one. William became *Duke of Normandy* at around seven years old.

A child. A bastard. A ruler. What followed was not a reign, but a siege.

Normandy descended into chaos. Powerful men saw opportunity. Guardians betrayed him. Noble families rose against him. His household was infiltrated. His tutors were murdered. More than once, *William* escaped assassination only because someone woke him in time.

At night, he was moved from castle to castle to avoid being killed in his sleep. This is what bastard hood meant in practice.

No assumption of protection. No inherited safety. No margin for weakness. William learned early that legitimacy was not something you possessed, it was something you had to enforce.

The boy did not grow soft. He grew watchful. By his teens, he was already hardened by instability. He learned to read threat, measure loyalty, and punish betrayal without hesitation. When rebellion came, and it came repeatedly, he crushed it with precision and brutality. Mercy, he understood, was a luxury afforded to the secure.

His bastard birth had taught him something the legitimate rarely learned: power is never given freely, it is taken, defended, and maintained.

By adulthood, William had secured Normandy. But security was not enough. Bastards are never allowed to remain merely adequate. Their legitimacy is always provisional.

So he aimed higher.

Across the Channel sat England, rich, divided, and ruled by a king with no clear heir. William claimed that the English crown had been promised to him. Whether that promise truly existed mattered less than this: he believed he had the right to take what had never been offered freely.

. . .

In 1066, William crossed the sea with an army. At the Battle of Hastings, he defeated and killed King Harold II. The victory was decisive, but not symbolic. *William* did not absorb England into Normandy. He dismantled its ruling class entirely. He replaced the Anglo-Saxon elite with Norman lords loyal only to him.

He redistributed land, crushed rebellion, and imposed a new order built on control, documentation, and fear. The Domesday Book, a vast record of land and wealth, was not administration. It was domination made permanent.

By conquest, William did what legitimacy had denied him.

He rewrote the hierarchy. His accomplishments were absolute:

- He conquered England and became its king
- He permanently transformed English aristocracy, land ownership, and governance
- He introduced Norman law, language, and culture
- He centralised royal authority beyond any previous English ruler
- He commissioned the Domesday Book, creating the most comprehensive record of medieval wealth and power

He founded a ruling dynasty that reshaped Britain for centuries

William ruled England not as a grateful recipient of legitimacy, but as someone who understood exactly how fragile legitimacy was, and how easily it could be replaced by force.

He never forgot what it meant to be a bastard.

His reign was efficient, strategic, and unforgiving. He trusted few. He rewarded loyalty precisely. He punished defiance completely. England under William was not gentle, but it was controlled.

In 1087, William died not in battle, but from injury sustained during a military campaign in France. Even in death, there was no softness. His body was too large for the stone tomb prepared for him. When it was forced inside, it split. The ceremony descended into disorder.

His burial was interrupted by a man claiming the land beneath the church had been stolen from his family — and demanding compensation before the king could be laid to rest.

Even at the end, William was contested. Even in death, legitimacy was not clean.

But history did not remember him as a bastard.

It remembered him as ***William the Conqueror***.

That is the failure of the sentence. The insult that was meant to diminish him became irrelevant. The status that was meant to contain him collapsed under the weight of what he built.

William did not overcome his bastard hood. He weaponised it.

And in doing so, he set the pattern that repeats throughout this book: when a child is denied legitimacy, some will break.

Others will comply. And a few, dangerously few, will decide that if the world will not recognise them, they will reshape the world until it has no choice.

William was the first. He was not the last.

A.Moreau

CHAPTER 2

ELIZABETH THE ERASED

DECLARED A BASTARD, RULED ANYWAY

Elizabeth was not born a bastard. She was made one. She entered the world in 1533 as the lawful daughter of King Henry VIII and Anne Boleyn, a marriage recognised by church and state. Cannon fire announced her birth. She was christened with ceremony. For a brief moment, she was England's legitimate heir.

Then her mother fell. Anne Boleyn was arrested, tried, and executed on charges designed to erase her, adultery, incest, treason. Within days, Henry annulled the marriage. With the stroke of legal authority, Elizabeth's status was rewritten.

She was declared illegitimate. Not because of how she was born, but because of how power chose to remember it.

Elizabeth was three years old when legitimacy was taken from her. Too young to understand the charge, old enough to live with the consequences. She was removed from court. Her household was reduced. Her title was stripped. She was no longer a princess, but *the king's daughter*, a semantic demotion with real force.

Her mother's name became dangerous to speak. Her own position became uncertain.

This was illegitimacy imposed after the fact, a reminder that for women, legitimacy is never fixed. It can be revoked by men, by law, by narrative.

Elizabeth grew up watching the ground shift beneath her. She saw her father marry again and again. She saw queens crowned and discarded. She saw siblings elevated and erased. She learned early that safety was provisional, and affection unreliable.

She learned to be careful. Elizabeth became observant, controlled, restrained. She learned languages. She learned history. She learned how power justified itself. She learned, above all, how to survive silence.

Her brother, Edward VI, restored her status partially, but not securely. Her sister Mary I later imprisoned her in the Tower of London, suspecting her of treason. Elizabeth was questioned, isolated, and kept under watch. She did not confess. She did not protest. She waited. Illegitimacy taught her patience.

When Mary died in 1558, Elizabeth ascended the throne, not as a cherished heir, but as a politically expedient one. Even as queen, her legitimacy remained fragile.

She was a woman in a man's office. She was unmarried.

She had no heir. Each of these facts was treated as a flaw. Together, they were seen as a liability. Parliament urged her to marry. Foreign powers sought to control her through marriage. Courtiers speculated about her body as if it were a matter of state. Elizabeth refused. Marriage, she understood, was another form of permission — one she did not intend to grant. She ruled alone.

Elizabeth built power not through inheritance or alliance, but through control. She centralised authority, balanced factions, and governed with calculated ambiguity. She learned when to speak, when to remain silent, and when to let others underestimate her.

Her illegitimacy — once a threat — became insulation.

She had no husband to dominate her. No son to replace her.

No lineage to protect. She ruled as someone with nothing to inherit and nothing to surrender.

Her accomplishments were decisive:

- She stabilised England after decades of religious turmoil
- She established a Protestant settlement that endured
- She defeated the Spanish Armada, preserving English sovereignty
- She strengthened royal authority while avoiding civil war
- She presided over a cultural renaissance in literature, theatre, and exploration
- She transformed England into a rising global power

Elizabeth ruled for forty-five years, longer than any of her immediate predecessors. Her reign became synonymous with strength, intelligence, and control.

But she was never allowed to forget how close she had come to erasure. She signed death warrants. She crushed rebellion. She tolerated no rival claims. Not out of cruelty, but memory. Elizabeth understood something legitimacy tries to hide: that power is not moral, only managed.

She died in 1603, unmarried and childless. With her death, the Tudor line ended. The legitimacy her father had obsessed over dissolved anyway.

What remained was her reign. History remembers Elizabeth not as illegitimate, but as **Elizabeth the Great.** That is the second failure of the sentence.

Illegitimacy was meant to weaken her claim. Instead, it freed her from the expectations that ruined others. Where legitimate heirs inherited obligation, Elizabeth inherited clarity.

She ruled without protection — and without permission.

And in doing so, she proved something this book returns to again and again: When legitimacy is unstable, some learn to cling to it.

Others learn to *outgrow it*. Elizabeth chose the latter.

CHAPTER 3

DON JUAN OF AUSTRIA THE HIDDEN

CONCEALED SON OF AN EMPEROR, UNLEASHED AS A WEAPON

Don Juan of Austria was born into the highest power in Europe — and denied it. He entered the world in 1547 as the illegitimate son of Emperor Charles V, ruler of the Holy Roman Empire and King of Spain. His mother was a woman of no political standing. Their relationship was concealed. The child was hidden. For years, his existence was managed as a problem rather than acknowledged as a fact.

Illegitimacy at this level was not sentimental. It was strategic.

Don Juan spent his early childhood moved between households, raised under assumed names, his identity carefully controlled. He was educated, disciplined, prepared, but never claimed.

He lived close enough to power to feel it, and far enough from legitimacy to know it would never be his.

When Charles V abdicated and died, Don Juan was still a boy. His half-brother, Philip II of Spain, inherited the empire, and with it, responsibility for the bastard he could not erase.

Philip acknowledged Don Juan publicly, but acknowledgment

was not elevation. Don Juan was given status, education, and opportunity, but never succession. The crown remained sealed.

The line was clear. This is how bastards are often managed: *useful, visible, but contained.*

Don Juan learned quickly that loyalty would not earn inheritance. His path to power lay elsewhere. He chose command.

Philip II placed him in military roles where success could be rewarded without threatening lineage. Don Juan embraced this fully. He trained obsessively, cultivated discipline, and pursued authority through competence rather than birthright.

He understood the terms of his existence: he would be allowed to serve, brilliantly, but never to rule. Illegitimacy clarifies ambition.

In 1571, Don Juan was appointed commander of the Holy League's naval forces against the Ottoman Empire. The stakes were enormous. Ottoman expansion threatened Christian control of the Mediterranean.

Failure would have reshaped Europe's balance of power.

Don Juan was twenty-four. At the ***Battle of Lepanto***, he led a coalition fleet into direct confrontation with the Ottomans.

The battle was brutal, chaotic, and decisive. Against expectation, the Holy League won a resounding victory, destroying much of the Ottoman navy.

It was one of the most significant naval battles in history. Europe celebrated. The Church exalted him. His name spread across the continent.

But celebration is not succession.

. . .

His accomplishments were unmistakable:

- He commanded the Holy League fleet at the Battle of Lepanto
- He delivered one of the Ottoman Empire's greatest military defeats
- He became Europe's most celebrated young commander
- He stabilised Mediterranean power at a critical moment
- He embodied imperial authority without holding a crown

Despite his victory, Don Juan remained structurally illegitimate. His fame made him valuable, and dangerous. Philip II grew wary of his popularity, his ambition, his independence. Bastards who succeed too visibly threaten the fiction that legitimacy equals authority.

Don Juan was reassigned. Contained. Watched. He was sent to govern the Spanish Netherlands, a region in rebellion. The position was unstable and thankless, an honour designed to fail quietly. Don Juan attempted negotiation, then force. Neither succeeded fully. Resources were limited. Support was conditional.

He was never given what he needed to rule effectively. Illegitimacy rarely grants margin.

In 1578, Don Juan died suddenly at the age of thirty-one, likely from typhus. He was young, celebrated, exhausted — and still excluded from the line that had produced him.

He left no heirs. He founded no dynasty. He wore no crown. History remembers him not as a claimant, but as a commander.

That is the shape bastard hood often takes near absolute power.

Don Juan was permitted glory, but not permanence. Authority, but not succession. Visibility, but not inheritance.

His life demonstrates a subtler cruelty than exile or erasure: proximity without belonging.

He was allowed to defend empire, never to inherit it.

That is the final lesson of *Kings Without Crowns*. Illegitimacy does not always deny access outright.

Sometimes it offers power carefully measured, so that nothing essential can be taken.

Don Juan of Austria did everything legitimacy demands, courage, loyalty, sacrifice, and was still denied its reward. Not because he failed. But because he was born. And that is the sentence this book begins by exposing.

SUMMARY PART I

KINGS WITHOUT CROWNS

Denied inheritance. Took power anyway

The opening movement of this book examines illegitimacy where it is most dangerous: at the edge of sovereignty. These chapters focus on individuals born close enough to power to threaten it, yet denied legitimacy by birth or decree. Their lives reveal how authority behaves when inheritance is withheld but capability remains.

William of Normandy was illegitimate by birth and marked as such from childhood. His claim to rule was contested from the moment it existed. Assassination attempts, betrayal, and instability shaped his early life. William learned that legitimacy would never be granted to him safely. His response was conquest. By force, he replaced lineage with domination, dismantling England's ruling class and rebuilding the hierarchy entirely. The insult attached to his name did not survive what he constructed.

Elizabeth Tudor was legitimate at birth and rendered illegitimate by political convenience. After her mother's execution, her status was erased retroactively, stripping her of security and protection. She grew up under constant threat, learning restraint rather than aggression. When she became queen, she ruled without the conventional shields of monarchy: no husband, no heir, no unquestioned claim. Elizabeth converted instability into control, governing through patience, calculation, and refusal to surrender authority. Her power lay not in conquest, but in endurance.

Don Juan of Austria was born the illegitimate son of the most powerful ruler in Europe, Emperor Charles V. His existence was concealed, then acknowledged, but never legitimised. Raised close to empire yet barred from inheritance, Don Juan was offered service instead of succession. He chose command as his path to authority. At twenty-four, he led the Holy League to a decisive victory over the Ottoman Empire at the Battle of Lepanto, reshaping the balance of power in the Mediterranean. Celebrated but contained, he was never allowed permanence. His fame made him useful, and therefore suspect. He died young, crowned with glory but denied lineage.

Together, these figures establish the book's first and most unforgiving argument: legitimacy is not synonymous with ability, loyalty, or achievement. It is a mechanism designed to protect continuity, not excellence.

When legitimacy is denied, power does not disappear.

It changes form. Some replace it with force. Some master its instability. Some are permitted to serve, brilliantly, but never to inherit.

Kings Without Crowns shows that bastard hood at the highest level produces not weakness, but adaptation.

These are not stories of rebellion for its own sake. They are records of how authority is taken, managed, or constrained when birth disqualifies but competence threatens.

This opening section establishes the pattern the book will follow: illegitimacy is not a personal failure. It is a structural sentence, and one that history repeatedly fails to enforce.

PART II

POWER WITHOUT PERMISSION

INTERLUDE PART II

POWER WITHOUT PERMISSION

Legitimacy is often spoken of as if it were a foundation—solid, inherited, permanent. But legitimacy is not strength. It is permission. And permission can be withdrawn.

The legitimate child grows up assuming stability. Their place is given, not earned. Their identity is constructed around assurances: of belonging, of continuity, of protection. But a life built on assurances is a life vulnerable to interruption.

When legitimacy is threatened, the legitimate often fracture.

They have been taught that identity is secured by birth, not by action. When the world contradicts that lesson—through loss, failure, or displacement—they face a form of disorientation unfamiliar to the illegitimate child, who learned from the beginning that nothing was guaranteed.

This is the quiet truth societies do not name: *Legitimacy creates dependency. Illegitimacy creates competence.*

The legitimate child is raised inside a structure that reflects them back to themselves with approval. The bastard child is raised in a world that offers no such mirror. One is affirmed; the other must construct their own reflection. One inherits a place; the other has to locate it. This difference is not moral. It is structural.

Legitimacy rests on external validation, lineage, marriage, tradition, law. When those structures shake, the legitimate feel the tremor in their core.

Illegitimate children, having built themselves without such scaffolding, are rarely shaken in the same way.

This is why history records so many illegitimate individuals rising under pressure: they have practiced survival their entire lives.

Their identity was never secured by circumstance, so circumstance cannot unmake it.

But legitimacy carries another fragility: *expectations*.

The legitimate are often told what they *should* become, what they *must* inherit, what they *owe* to a name or a lineage.

These expectations can be as heavy as any stigma.

Illegitimate children, by contrast, inherit no blueprint. Their lives are defined less by obligation and more by possibility.

This is the irony institutions avoid acknowledging:

The child born into legitimacy is often more constrained than the child born without it.

Legitimacy promises protection, but it also limits motion. Illegitimacy offers no protection, but it frees the child from the weight of inherited purpose. And once that child discovers direction, their momentum is their own.

This interlude does not argue that legitimate children are weak. It argues that the category itself is fragile, dependent on continuity, recognition, and compliance.

Illegitimacy survives violation. Legitimacy does not.

In the chapters ahead, you will see this pattern again: those raised outside the structures of approval discover capacities those inside them rarely need to develop.

Legitimacy rests on order. Illegitimacy grows through adaptation.

And adaptation, in the long arc of history, is the more enduring force.

CHAPTER 4

LEONARDO THE UNCLAIMED

BORN OUTSIDE MARRIAGE, CLAIMED ONLY BY GENIUS

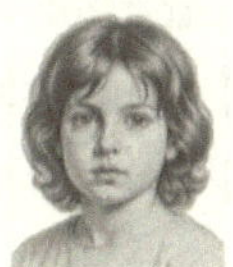

Leonardo was not born into rebellion. He was born into exclusion. He entered the world in 1452 in Vinci, a small Tuscan town, the illegitimate son of Ser Piero da Vinci, a notary of some standing, and Caterina, a peasant woman whose life disappears almost entirely from the historical record.

His father acknowledged him, but did not legitimate him. Leonardo was taken into his father's household, yet remained marked as separate, present, but never fully claimed.

Illegitimacy placed him in a narrow space: too connected to be abandoned, too illegitimate to be inherited. That space would shape everything. As an illegitimate child, Leonardo was barred from the formal education that defined the Renaissance elite.

He could not attend university. He could not train as a lawyer, a notary, or a physician. He was excluded from the intellectual inheritance of Europe, from classical languages, scholastic philosophy, and institutional theology.

This mattered more than poverty would have. Leonardo was not denied comfort. He was denied *credentialed authority*.

He grew up without the scaffolding that told other men what knowledge mattered and what questions were permissible.

Instead, he was apprenticed to a workshop — trained to observe, copy, grind pigments, prepare surfaces, and watch the world closely. Illegitimacy did not place him below knowledge. It placed him outside it. And so he learned differently.

Leonardo trusted what he could see. He watched muscles move beneath skin. He watched water curl around obstacles. He watched birds rise and fall on currents of air.

Where scholars debated Aristotle, Leonardo opened bodies.

Where theologians argued first causes, Leonardo measured effects.

This was not defiance. It was adaptation.

Denied formal instruction, he built his own education, one grounded in observation, experiment, and relentless curiosity.

He kept notebooks obsessively, filling them with questions rather than conclusions. His pages are crowded, restless, unfinished. He did not seek closure. He sought understanding.

Leonardo moved freely between disciplines because no institution had taught him they were separate. Painting led naturally to anatomy. Anatomy to mechanics. Mechanics to flight. Flight to geometry. Geometry back to art.

Legitimacy teaches hierarchy. Illegitimacy dissolves it. Leonardo's illegitimate status also shaped his relationship to authority.

He did not write treatises intended for publication. He did not argue publicly with scholars. He did not seek to found a school or gather disciples.

He worked quietly, often privately, producing knowledge without demanding recognition.

This distance from authority was not humility. It was autonomy.

His art reflects this independence. His figures are not symbols. They are bodies, weighted, balanced, anatomically precise. Faces are not idealised; they are restrained, inward, difficult to read.

Emotion is present, but controlled. Nothing is overstated.

Even *The Last Supper*, a religious subject, is treated as a study of human reaction rather than divine revelation.

The miracle is not at the centre. The people are. Leonardo did not decorate doctrine. He interrogated reality.

His accomplishments were singular and cumulative:

- He transformed painting through mastery of anatomy, perspective, light, and composition.
- He created works that remain central to global culture, including *The Last Supper* and *Mona Lisa.*
- He pioneered anatomical study through direct dissection and scientific illustration.
- He advanced understanding of optics, engineering, hydraulics, and mechanics.
- He designed conceptual machines centuries ahead of their time, including flying devices and military engines.
- He left notebooks that redefined how knowledge could

be pursued — experimentally, visually, without permission.

Leonardo never married. He never secured permanent institutional patronage. He moved between courts and cities, valued for his mind but never fully absorbed into any system. He belonged everywhere temporarily and nowhere completely.

This too was bastard hood. Unlike William or Napoleon, Leonardo did not seek to dominate the world. He sought to understand it. But the root was the same: a life lived without inherited permission. He was not bound to tradition because tradition had never claimed him.

Leonardo died in 1519 in France, under the patronage of King Francis I, who admired him not as a scholar or courtier, but as something rarer, a mind unconfined by category. According to tradition, he died quietly, his notebooks still unfinished, his questions still open.

History does not remember ***Leonardo*** as illegitimate. It remembers him as ***genius***. That is another failure of the sentence.

Illegitimacy was meant to limit him. Instead, it removed the constraints that produce imitation. Where legitimacy teaches continuity, exclusion can produce originality.

Leonardo did not inherit a worldview. He constructed one, patiently, obsessively, without asking permission. And in doing so, he proved that when authority is denied, creation itself can become a form of sovereignty.

CHAPTER 5

ALEXANDER HAMILTON THE UNLAWFUL

FORBIDDEN CHILD, ARCHITECT OF A NATION

Alexander Hamilton was born without a name that could protect him. He entered the world around 1755 on the Caribbean island of Nevis, the illegitimate son of a Scottish trader and a woman trapped in an abusive marriage. His parents were not married.

Under the law, that fact erased him. He could not inherit. He could not claim legitimacy through his father. He did not properly belong to either parent's world. Then his father disappeared.

Hamilton was still a boy when abandonment became permanent. His mother died soon after, leaving him orphaned and legally unrecognised. He was taken in by relatives who had no obligation to keep him. His education was improvised. His future uncertain.

This was illegitimacy at its most complete: no lineage, no protection, no guaranteed place. Hamilton learned early that survival depended on usefulness.

He worked as a clerk for a trading company, mastering accounts, correspondence, and logistics. Numbers became order. Order became safety. In a world where people vanished, systems endured.

A hurricane devastated the island in 1772. Hamilton wrote about it — not sentimentally, but with precision and force. His words impressed local patrons enough to fund his education abroad.

It was an accidental rescue. And he never trusted accidents again.

Hamilton arrived in North America carrying nothing but urgency. He studied relentlessly. When revolution came, he attached himself to it not out of romance, but recognition. Upheaval creates space for those with no inheritance.

He distinguished himself quickly, through competence, discipline, and an intolerance for chaos.

George Washington noticed. Hamilton became his aide-de-camp, absorbing power at close range, learning how authority functions when everything is unstable.

Hamilton did not dream of freedom. He dreamed of permanence. After independence, the new United States was fragile, indebted, and divided. Many celebrated the collapse of monarchy.

Hamilton saw something else: the risk of disintegration. He understood what happens when systems fail. He had lived it.

So he set about building what he had never been given.

- His accomplishments were foundational:

- He was the principal architect of the American financial system
- He established a national bank and public credit
- He organised federal taxation and debt assumption
- He co-authored *The Federalist Papers*, shaping constitutional interpretation
- He strengthened executive power to stabilise the state
- He built institutions designed to outlast personalities

Hamilton believed legitimacy should be institutional, not inherited. Law, credit, and structure would replace bloodline and name. Where others feared centralisation, he saw continuity. Where others trusted virtue, he trusted design. This made him controversial. And dangerous.

Hamilton provoked enemies easily. He was impatient, combative, and unwilling to soften his positions. Bastards often are. When you begin without protection, compromise feels like exposure.

His personal life remained unsettled. He married and had children, but never escaped scrutiny. His affair with Maria Reynolds was exposed publicly, and Hamilton, obsessed with control of narrative, confessed in detail rather than allow speculation.

It was a familiar pattern: tell the truth before others weaponise it.

Hamilton's death was sudden and public. In 1804, he was shot in a duel by Aaron Burr, a political rival. He died the following day.

He was forty-nine years old. At the time of his death, he was widely disliked. His ideas were contested. His temperament was resented. He did not live to see his system vindicated. But the system endured.

American finance, governance, and constitutional interpretation continue to bear his imprint. The permanence he sought outlived him, exactly as he intended.

Hamilton's illegitimacy was not a footnote. It was the source of his obsession. He did not seek acceptance. He sought structure.

Where others inherited legitimacy, *Hamilton* manufactured it, not for himself, but for a nation that, like him, had been born without precedent and without protection.

That is another failure of the sentence.

Illegitimacy was meant to marginalise him. Instead, it trained him to think beyond personality, beyond approval, beyond name. Hamilton did not rise above his origins. He built a system so strong that origins stopped mattering.

CHAPTER 6

T. E. LAWRENCE THE UNNAMED

ILLEGITIMATE BY SECRECY, LOYAL TO NO INHERITANCE

Thomas Edward Lawrence was born into a secret. His mother had been a governess. His father, Sir Thomas Chapman, abandoned his wife and legitimate daughters to live with her under false names.

They called themselves "Mr. and Mrs. Lawrence," moving often, carrying the weight of exposure wherever they went. *T. E.* Lawrence grew up knowing that his existence was something to be concealed, rearranged, explained only in fragments.

Illegitimacy shaped his life long before he had language for it. There was no inheritance awaiting him, no family line to extend, no name secure enough to claim publicly.

Everything in his life was provisional: their identity, their home, their social status. He grew up inside a structure that could collapse at the slightest inquiry.

The lesson was simple, and it stayed with him forever: Belonging could vanish at any moment. He responded the way illegitimate minds often do: by learning to live everywhere, and nowhere.

Lawrence moved through the world as an observer first. He studied landscapes, ruins, languages, and people with an intensity born not of curiosity alone, but of survival.

When you grow up in a life held together by secrecy, you learn to see what others overlook. You notice the shift in tone, the nuance in alliances, the invisible boundaries that separate one world from another.

Lawrence became fluent in difference. It became his greatest weapon. At Oxford, he excelled not through pedigree but through precision. His scholarship on medieval castles was meticulous, unusual, and strangely intimate for a boy without a solid home.

He understood fortifications because he understood the need for them—not in stone, but in life. His entry into the Arab world was not a departure from his identity. It was an extension of it.

Lawrence did not arrive in Arabia as a conqueror. He arrived as a listener. He respected the cultures he encountered, learned the dialects, and adapted himself to the rhythms of desert life.

He grew close to tribal leaders not through rank but through trust, a trust earned quietly, through attention and humility. He belonged there, not because he was one of them, but because he never pretended to be.

A man with no stable identity moves easily among those who define identity differently.

During the Arab Revolt of 1916–1918, Lawrence became a force that Britain could not understand and Arabia could not fully contain.

He advised, negotiated, and strategised with an instinct sharpened by a lifetime of reading the unspoken.

While British officers relied on hierarchy, Lawrence relied on perception.

He understood loyalty not as duty but as choice. He understood legitimacy not as birthright but as recognition. He understood power not as possession but as persuasion. He fought not for empire, but for the promise he believed the British had made to the Arab world—and would later betray.

This betrayal marked him. He had grown up inside a lie; now he witnessed one on a global scale. After the war, Lawrence became famous. A legend. A myth. And he hated it. Illegitimate children learn early that visibility is danger.

Lawrence understood this too well. He spent the rest of his life trying to disappear. He changed names repeatedly. He enlisted in the Royal Air Force under false identities. He rejected promotions and recognition.

He refused every attempt to turn him into a symbol. He knew that the narrative others built around him was a form of possession, a claim he did not want and never trusted.

His death in 1935—after a motorcycle crash near his cottage, was quiet, sudden, and strangely fitting.

A man who belonged everywhere and nowhere left the world without ceremony, without heirs, without lineage, without a name secure enough to bind him.

What remains of Lawrence is not the myth, but the pattern:

- A child raised under a false identity becomes a man fluent in shifting allegiances.

- A boy taught to hide becomes a strategist who understands the cost of visibility.
- A life without belonging becomes a mind that sees through the illusions of empire, nation, and legitimacy itself.

Lawrence understood what many legitimate men never learn: when you are born outside the protections of a system, you see the system clearly. And clarity is its own form of power.

He built no dynasty. He inherited nothing. He left behind no descendants to carry a name he never truly had. But he altered a region, a revolt, a narrative of empire.

He proved that influence does not require permission; it requires perception. And that a man with no rightful place can shape the destiny of places that were never meant to be his.

SUMMARY PART II

POWER WITHOUT PERMISSION

This section examines three figures who were denied formal legitimacy yet reshaped the world through intellect, invention, and strategic clarity.

None inherited power. None entered systems designed to accept them. Their influence came from the perspective of the outsider, the ability to see what those born inside structures of legitimacy could not.

Leonardo da Vinci began life as a literal bastard, barred from classical education and excluded from the elite professions of his time. What he lacked in institutional access he replaced with curiosity sharpened by distance. Because he did not inherit the accepted frameworks of knowledge, he built his own. His notebooks, restless, precise, unbound by convention, represent the creativity of someone unconfined by inherited thinking. Leonardo did not work within the systems of his era; he quietly transcended them.

Alexander Hamilton was illegitimate by every measure: born out of wedlock in poverty, orphaned, denied the protections and expectations of legitimate sons. But illegitimacy gave him a ferocious clarity about power, who held it, how it moved, and how it could be built from nothing. In the United States, he engineered financial and constitutional structures that outlast all their creators. Hamilton is the clearest example of a man who, denied a place in society, constructed one for the entire nation.

T. E. Lawrence, born to unmarried parents living under false names, grew up in a world where identity was fragile and belonging conditional. This early instability trained him in perception—reading rooms, cultures, and allegiances with uncommon sensitivity. In Arabia, he built alliances through understanding rather than rank, wielding influence that confounded the British Empire. Lawrence's power came not from authority but from insight: the acute vision of someone who never fully belonged anywhere.

Together, these three form a single argument: illegitimacy sharpens vision. Exclusion refines intellect. Being denied permission teaches a person how to move without it.

Part II shows that some of history's greatest creators, architects, and strategists were shaped not by acceptance, but by the absence of it. What legitimacy grants in comfort, illegitimacy grants in clarity—and clarity, in the hands of the outsider, becomes power.

PART III

WOMEN WITHOUT PROTECTION

INTERLUDE PART III

WOMEN WITHOUT PROTECTION

Inheritance, Permission, and Self-Invention

Illegitimate children learn early that the world does not hand them a script.

They grow without the assurances legitimate children mistake for identity: inheritance, protection, expectation, a place prepared in advance. Their lives require invention. Not reinvention, not recovery, invention from the beginning.

Inheritance gives shape. Illegitimacy gives blankness. Blankness can be frightening. But it can also be liberating.

Those denied a predetermined path discover, often painfully, that they must construct their own. They learn to read systems rather than belong to them, to build rather than inherit, to question rather than accept. The mind grows sharper in places where permission is withheld. But a deeper truth emerges at the end of this section: exclusion is not experienced equally.

Leonardo, *Hamilton*, and *Lawrence* were denied legitimacy by birth, class, secrecy, or social order. They built influence through intellect, invention, and strategic clarity. Yet each moved through a world that still granted them one unspoken privilege:

They were men. For all their exclusion, they were not excluded from possibility itself.

Their ambitions, unconventional as they were, could still expand outward, into studios of patronage, new nations, military command. They fought to enter systems that resisted them, but the systems existed. The gates were closed, but visible. For *women*, the gates were not only closed. Often, they were invisible. Illegitimacy for women carried a second sentence: gender.

Where men might reinvent themselves, women were expected to disappear. Where men could turn exclusion into ambition, women were expected to absorb it quietly, without rebellion, without movement. A man born illegitimate might rise through talent.

A woman born illegitimate, or merely unprotected, was expected to be grateful simply to survive. The next part of this book turns to those women. Women whose illegitimacy was compounded by the structures built to confine them. Women who were denied protection, denied permission, denied place, not because of what they were born into, but because of what they were born as.

Their identities were not only unsanctioned. Their existence was regulated. Yet they built lives, careers, and worlds anyway, not by stepping into systems from the side, as men sometimes could, but by creating space where none was offered. Their self-invention was not ambition. It was survival.

Part III follows those women, not as footnotes or exceptions, but as evidence that exclusion, multiplied, does not silence the illegitimate mind. It intensifies it.

CHAPTER 7

EVA PERÓN THE UNACKNOWLEDGED

DENIED AT BIRTH, EMBRACED BY MILLIONS

Eva Duarte was born on the wrong side of a line she did not draw. Her father, Juan Duarte, had a legitimate family in the city and an illegitimate one in the countryside. He supported both until the moment he didn't.

When he died, the legitimate family barred the illegitimate from the funeral. The young Eva, dressed in her best, was refused entry. She stood outside and watched the family he chose mourn the man who had denied her.

This was her first public lesson in legitimacy: *that the law protects the powerful, not the innocent.*

Eva grew up in poverty, surrounded by absence.

There was no inheritance to claim, no name that carried weight, no shield from judgment. In rural Argentina, illegitimacy was not simply a social mark; it was a moral one. It meant impurity. It meant that the hierarchy of birth had already made its decision about her.

She understood early that if she wanted a place in the world, she would have to invent it.

At fifteen, she left home for Buenos Aires, a city where women like her were expected to vanish into factories, brothels, or the invisible margins. She arrived with no protection, no money, and no legitimate claim to prospects. But illegitimate children learn quickly to find openings where others see walls.

Eva pushed her way into acting, radio, and the small constellation of Argentine celebrity. She was mocked for her ambition. For her poverty. For her unknown father. The elite treated her as a pretender, someone who belonged at the edges, not the centre.

But illegitimacy teaches defiance.

Eva did not soften her accent, erase her past, or seek acceptance from the families who dismissed her.

She spoke to those who had lived the sentence she had lived: people without names, without assets, without recognition. People who were workers, migrants, or illegitimate in the broader social order of Argentina.

When she met Juan Perón, she did not step into legitimacy. She stepped into power. Eva understood something Perón did not: the emotional architecture of exclusion. She knew what humiliation felt like.

She knew the violence of being denied dignity. She could speak to the poor, the forgotten, the unprotected—not as a benefactor, but as one of them.

She built a new identity for herself and, in the process, helped construct a new political identity for the nation.

Where others saw a bastard child from the provinces, she saw a constituency. Where elites saw a threat, she saw a foundation.

Where society tried to shame her, she refused to bow. Her speeches were not elegant. They were effective. Not polished. True. Not conciliatory. Direct.

She understood something the legitimate classes never grasped: *people do not want permission. They want recognition.*

In her work with labor unions, with women's suffrage, with the poor, she created a political language grounded in belonging rather than birth. It was radical not because it promised equality, but because it suggested legitimacy itself was a fiction.

And the elites despised her for it. They called her a whore. A fraud. A social climber. A bastard. The words meant to wound her only confirmed her power.

Eva Perón was the illegitimate woman who forced a country built on European hierarchy to look directly at its own hypocrisy.

She understood that shame is inherited only by those who accept it, and she refused.

When she died in 1952, at thirty-three, she was mourned by millions. The poor lined the streets for days.

The same elites who had mocked her debated how to handle her body, as if they feared she might rise again. Her corpse became a political object, hidden, stolen, moved across continents, denied peace even in death.

Her illegitimacy followed her beyond the grave, not as disgrace, but as threat. Eva Perón had done something few illegitimate women in history achieved: she inverted the hierarchy.

She turned the stigma of her origin into a weapon. She took a place the world tried to forbid. She became the symbolic mother of a nation that once denied her the right to mourn her own father.

Her power did not come from marriage. It did not come from beauty. It did not come from politics.

It came from the clarity that only an illegitimate child acquires: *If the world refuses to grant you legitimacy, you take authority instead.*

Eva Perón did not ask to belong. She claimed the nation that excluded her.

And in doing so, she proved that legitimacy is not inherited—it is constructed, contested, and, sometimes, conquered.

CHAPTER 8

COCO CHANEL THE UNANCHORED

ABANDONED GIRL WHO REDEFINED FEMININITY

Gabrielle Chanel was born without protection. She entered the world in 1883 in Saumur, France, the illegitimate child of a market trader and a laundress. Her parents were not married. Her mother died when Gabrielle was young. Her father did not stay. He delivered his daughters to an orphanage and disappeared from their lives.

There was no explanation. No ceremony. No return. Illegitimacy, in this form, is abandonment made permanent.

The convent at Aubazine offered order, not affection. The girls were clothed, fed, instructed, and erased. Uniformity replaced individuality. Silence was enforced. Desire was disciplined out of view. Femininity was defined as obedience.

Chanel absorbed the lesson and rejected its conclusion. She learned to sew. She learned restraint. She learned how women were expected to take up as little space as possible. She also learned how fragile protection was, and how quickly it could be withdrawn. She would not depend on it again.

When Chanel left the orphanage, she entered a world that offered women only a few sanctioned futures. Marriage. Domesticity. Dependence. For an illegitimate woman without dowry or name, even those options were narrow.

So she improvised. She worked as a seamstress. She sang in cafés. She moved through relationships with men who could offer access, but not ownership. She understood power before she possessed it. She learned how proximity worked, and how easily it failed.

Illegitimacy sharpens this awareness. Chanel did not romanticise poverty or submission. She observed women's lives with precision and impatience. She saw how clothing restricted movement, enforced class, and advertised dependency. Corsets, ornament, and fragility were not aesthetics to her. They were instructions. She dismantled them.

Chanel's designs were austere, functional, and modern. She borrowed from men's clothing not as imitation, but as theft. Comfort became radical. Simplicity became defiance. She dressed women for movement, work, and autonomy rather than display.

This was not fashion as decoration. It was fashion as refusal. Her accomplishments changed how women lived:

- She liberated women from restrictive clothing
- She redefined elegance as simplicity and function
- She introduced the Little Black Dress as modern uniform
- She built a fashion house controlled by a woman
- She transformed personal style into personal authority

Chanel understood something legitimacy-dependent designers rarely grasp: that respectability follows power, not the other way around. She did not wait to be accepted. She made herself necessary. Her personal life remained complicated and often morally ambiguous.

She aligned herself with powerful men. She made choices that would later be criticised and re-examined. Illegitimacy does not produce saints. It produces survivors.

Chanel did not seek redemption. She sought independence. She died in 1971, alone in a hotel room in Paris, still in control of her image, her brand, her space. The orphan who was never supposed to matter left behind one of the most enduring cultural empires of the twentieth century.

History does not remember Gabrielle Chanel as illegitimate.

It remembers her as *Coco Chanel.* That is the cost legitimacy never accounts for. When women are denied protection, they do not always break. Some rebuild the world so protection is no longer required.

Chanel did not ask to be sheltered. She dressed women to stand on their own.

CHAPTER 9

MARILYN MONROE THE UNPROTECTED

BORN WITHOUT A FATHER, CONSUMED BY VISIBILITY

Marilyn Monroe began life as a question. She was born in Los Angeles in 1926 as Norma Jeane Mortensen. No father was listed on the birth certificate. Different men were named at different times, none conclusively. Her mother, Gladys, was mentally unstable and financially fragile. Her father, whoever he was, never acknowledged her.

Illegitimacy was not a technicality. It was her beginning.

As a child, Norma Jeane lived in foster homes, rented rooms, and institutions. There was no stability, no money, no family name to shield her. She learned early that adults could disappear without explanation, and that safety depended on remaining agreeable.

This is the first lesson of female illegitimacy: when protection is absent, compliance becomes survival.

At one point, she lived with a family who planned to adopt her, but they never completed the process. Adoption papers were drawn up, then withdrawn. She remained unclaimed, in the limbo between belonging and rejection.

Norma Jeane learned not to expect permanence. Only change.

At sixteen, to escape the foster system and avoid returning to an orphanage, she married a neighbour's son. Not out of romance, but necessity.

It was her first reminder that marriage could function as a legal shelter — a substitute for the protection she had never been given. But protection through marriage is unstable.

It can be rescinded at any moment.

When her husband deployed overseas during the war, she was left alone again. She worked in a factory, where her photograph was taken for an army publication.

That image led to modelling, which led to acting, which led to a new name: *Marilyn Monroe.*

The reinvention was not vanity. It was strategy.

Marilyn built a persona capable of attracting attention, because attention was the only reliable form of protection available to women without class, family, or legitimacy.

She understood that visibility could be a shield, even if it was a fragile one. Hollywood sexualised her. Controlled her. Mocked her intelligence.

The studios dictated her contracts, her image, her salary, all at the lowest tier. She was valuable but not valued.

They used her beauty while disregarding the instability underneath it.

Marilyn understood the transaction. She just had no alternative.

Her achievements were significant:

- She became one of the most recognisable cultural figures of the 20th century
- She starred in films that defined an era, including Some Like It Hot, The Seven Year Itch, and Gentlemen Prefer Blondes
- She formed her own production company, rare for any actor, unprecedented for a woman of her time
- She developed a disciplined approach to acting, studying with Lee Strasberg and challenging assumptions about her artistry
- She transformed vulnerability into a performance language recognised worldwide

But the lack of protection never left her.

Even at the peak of fame, she was treated as decorative rather than autonomous. Newspapers published rumours about her morality. Studio executives dismissed her when she asked for better roles. Men desired her, possessed her, and abandoned her. The public adored her image while ignoring the person behind it.

Her marriages to Joe DiMaggio and Arthur Miller, repeated the same pattern: admiration that became control, affection that became scrutiny, intimacy that could not provide safety.

Marilyn's death in 1962, at just thirty-six, was the final expression of a life lived in the open without walls. The exact circumstances remain debated, but the deeper truth is clear:

She died as she lived, unprotected. Alone in a house that felt temporary.

Surrounded by people who needed her more than they guarded her. Supported by fame, not security.

Legitimate to the world, illegitimate to the structures that shaped her life.

Marilyn Monroe is often remembered as a symbol of glamour, tragedy, sexuality, or innocence.

But in the context of this book, she represents something more precise: she was a woman born without legitimacy who built global recognition out of sheer visibility — and paid the price for the world's inability to see beyond the image it demanded of her.

Illegitimacy was meant to mark her as lesser. It marked her as vulnerable. And vulnerability, in a woman, is easily exploited.

Marilyn did not overcome the sentence of illegitimacy through power or conquest. She resisted it through reinvention, again and again, until the reinvention consumed her.

History remembers her not as Norma Jeane, not as the unwanted child, not as the unprotected woman.

It remembers her as ***Marilyn Monroe***, an identity she created because the world never offered her one that was safe.

That is the tragedy and the defiance of her story.

HOLLYWOOD
HOLLYWOOD
CAPITOL

SUMMARY PART III

WOMEN WITHOUT PROTECTION

Illegitimacy multiplied. Ambition denied permission.

Part III examines a form of illegitimacy that is older than law and more enduring than lineage: the illegitimacy imposed on women through the absence of protection.

For men, illegitimacy usually concerns birth, inheritance, or legal status.

For women, it is compounded by gender, by the expectation of obedience, purity, and silence. A woman may be declared illegitimate not only because of who her parents were, but because of who she is, what she becomes, or what society demands she should not be.

Eva Perón, Coco Chanel, and Marilyn Monroe were shaped by this second sentence. They came from different countries, different eras, and different forms of abandonment, yet each of them entered the world without the safeguards society promises legitimate children. And each learned, in her own way, that self-invention was the only viable form of protection available to women without lineage, resources, or permission.

Eva Perón was marked by illegitimacy from birth, denied by her father's family, excluded from his funeral, and dismissed by the Argentine elite as someone who did not belong. She transformed exclusion into political presence, building a legitimacy rooted not in law but in devotion. She became the voice of those who, like her, had been unprotected by class and gender.

Coco Chanel was abandoned to a convent after her mother's death, raised in institutional austerity that erased identity as efficiently as poverty. She remade herself through discipline, invention, and clarity of aesthetic ambition. Chanel understood that femininity was both a constraint and an opportunity, and she rebuilt it entirely, not from privilege but from a life lived without safety.

Marilyn Monroe was born without a father's name, moved between foster homes, and left unshielded in a world that commodified beauty and ignored vulnerability. She created a persona powerful enough to eclipse the instability beneath it, turning absence into visibility. Yet the protection that fame promised never came; her life and death reveal how thoroughly the unprotected woman is still exposed.

Together, these women illustrate the thesis of Part III: When women are denied protection, they do not vanish. They construct identities powerful enough to replace the protection withheld from them. Their stories are not exceptions; they are evidence.

They show that female illegitimacy, whether by birth, class, gender, or desire, does not diminish capability. It intensifies invention. It forces clarity. It produces forms of power legitimacy cannot predict.

Part III stands as proof that the world's attempt to confine women through illegitimacy did not weaken them. It created forces it could not control.

The women in this section did not inherit safety, legitimacy, or place. They built what they needed from whatever the world withheld. Their power was not granted; it was constructed, quietly, strategically, and often at great cost.

They were not protected by the systems that claimed to define worth, yet they left marks deeper than those who were. Their stories reveal a simple truth: when the world denies legitimacy to a woman, it often creates the very force it fears.

Part III ends here, with women who refused disappearance.

Part IV begins with the modern world, where the sentence survives, but its consequences have changed shape, and its subjects have learned new ways to outgrow it.

PART IV

WHAT THE BASTARD OWES

INTERLUDE PART IV

WHAT THE BASTARD OWES

Illegitimacy begins as an accusation.

Not against the parents, who chose, acted, desired, but against the child, who did nothing.

The world implies that the bastard owes something for the circumstances of their birth: humility, gratitude, restraint. They are expected to live smaller, quieter, more grateful lives. To accept exclusion as natural. To repay a debt they never incurred.

But illegitimate children learn something society rarely anticipates:

they owe nothing. Not innocence. Not apology.

Not compliance with the structures that tried to contain them.

What they learn instead is how to build without inheritance, how to act without permission, how to create in the absence of guarantees. Where legitimacy offers a ready-made script, illegitimacy offers blankness, and blankness forces invention.

Yet as these lives unfold, a paradox emerges.

Those who owe the world the least often give it the most.

Not because they are virtuous. Not because they are grateful. But because the very conditions meant to diminish them sharpen something essential: clarity, autonomy, ambition, independence.

Illegitimate children do not inherit the world. So they remake it.

Charlie Chaplin took poverty, abandonment, and stigma and turned them into a universal language, comedy built from hunger, resilience shaped in alleys and workhouses.

Oprah Winfrey turned silence and invisibility into voice and authority, creating a platform the world had never seen from someone the world never expected to hear.

Steve Jobs turned relinquishment into an obsession with creation, a determination to build objects, systems, and worlds that did not yet exist, as if inventing the life he had not been handed.

None of them asked permission. None of them were granted legitimacy. All of them changed the world.

This interlude marks the final turn of the book: from illegitimacy as a historical sentence, to illegitimacy as a modern force , one that no longer seeks acceptance, no longer apologises for origin, no longer negotiates with systems that refused to recognise it.

The question of this section is not what the bastard owes.

The real question is what the world owes those it tried to exclude, and what it became because they refused to stay outside.

CHAPTER 10

CHARLIE CHAPLIN THE UNSHIELDED

ILLEGITIMATE CHILD OF POVERTY, PROTECTED BY PERFORMANCE

Charlie Chaplin was born into absence. His mother, Hannah, was an unwed music-hall performer, struggling with poverty and instability. His father, Charles Sr., was a singer who denied paternity, drank himself into irrelevance, and died young.

Chaplin grew up with no legitimate claim to a name, a home, a protector, or a future.

He began life on the margins of London's poorest streets, workhouses, charity homes, institutional beds. His illegitimacy was not just a private fact; it was a public condition. To be born outside marriage in Victorian England was to be marked. A child of no recognised father was expected to disappear into the lower classes without trace.

Chaplin refused disappearance. But first, he survived.

His childhood was defined by silence: his mother's voice fading into mental illness, his father's voice absent entirely, and society's voice telling him that a child like him was destined for labour, not expression.

Illegitimate children learn early that visibility is dangerous and that approval is conditional. Chaplin learned both truths before he could read.

He developed the instincts of the bastard mind: the ability to assess a room instantly, the sensitivity to shifts in tone, the hunger to matter, and the capacity to self-invent because no one else was going to define him.

Onstage, he discovered something astonishing: when he performed, the sentence lifted. The audience did not care who his father was.

They did not care what the church or the law called him. They cared that he could make them feel something.

Chaplin understood this difference. He understood that legitimacy is meaningless to people who are hurting. He understood that laughter can dismantle social hierarchy in a way moral lectures never could.

His rise was not an accident of talent. It was the revenge of a child who had been silenced.

In America, Chaplin created The Tramp, a figure of wandering poverty, loneliness, resilience, and quiet rebellion.

The Tramp is not comedic relief; he is autobiography. A man whose identity is unstable, whose place is temporary, whose dignity must be defended against a world that does not see him.

The Tramp is Chaplin's illegitimacy made visible. He is the global symbol of the unwanted child surviving by wit, softness, and defiance.

He is what Chaplin might have become if he had not found escape through performance: a man walking without destination, invented moment by moment, living outside the lines of acceptance.

Chaplin built an empire from nothing, the most recognised face on earth during the silent-film era. His success was the most public reminder that legitimacy predicts nothing. But even as he conquered cinema, his illegitimacy followed him in another form.

America loved Chaplin the clown. It feared Chaplin the thinker. His political views, his anti-authoritarian instincts, his distrust of institutions , all were natural extensions of the illegitimate child who had never known protection.

Chaplin saw how power disguised itself as morality, how conformity demanded silence, how respectability punished those born outside its narrow lines.

He refused to comply. The United States government retaliated by branding him a threat. A foreigner. A moral danger. An outsider who did not belong, the same accusation that had chased him since birth. Ultimately, America barred him from returning in 1952, exiling a man who had defined its early cinematic imagination.

Illegitimacy is not erased by success; it is amplified by it.

Chaplin spent his final decades in Switzerland, wealthy but still fundamentally rootless. He had built a global legacy, but belonging never settled fully upon him.

His life remained shaped by the instability of his origin, by a father who denied him, a mother who faded into illness, and a society that marked him as less before he had a chance to speak. Yet Chaplin's genius came not despite this fracture, but through it. His films gave voice to people who had none.

His characters dignified the poor, the abandoned, the illegitimate.

His comedy revealed the cruelty of systems built on hierarchy.

He was not a creator of jokes; he was an architect of empathy.

He made the world look at the unwanted child and laugh, not at him, but with him.

Charlie Chaplin died in 1977. His coffin was stolen by grave, robbers seeking ransom, one final violation of a life marked by instability. But even this grim episode reflected the truth of his existence: ***the world tried to possess him because it never succeeded in defining him.***

Today, Chaplin is remembered not for his shame, but for his capacity to transform it.

He proved that illegitimacy cannot silence a mind that invents itself. He proved that abandonment does not prevent creation. He proved that the child who grows up with nothing can teach the world how to feel. Chaplin belonged nowhere. Which is why his work belonged everywhere.

CHARLIE Chaplin
in MODERN TIMES
Written, Directed and Produced by CHARLES CHAPLIN

CHAPTER 11

STEVE JOBS THE UNCHOSEN

GIVEN AWAY AT BIRTH, FORCED THE WORLD TO CHOOSE HIM

Steve Jobs was born into contradiction. His biological parents—an unmarried Syrian Muslim student and a young American woman, conceived him in a world where their union was unacceptable. Marriage was impossible. Legitimacy unattainable. The solution, as society understood it, was removal: the child would be given away, his birth erased, his identity reassigned.

Jobs began life as an inconvenience to be managed.

Adoption softened the discomfort for the adults, not for the child. He entered a new family with new parents and a new name, but the fracture remained. Jobs spent his life navigating two origins: the one he came from and the one he was told to accept. Like many illegitimate or adopted children, he grew up with an unspoken contradiction: gratitude was expected; belonging was conditional.

He understood early that he had been chosen, but also that he had been relinquished.

This duality became the architecture of his mind.

Jobs developed the classic instincts of the illegitimate child:

a fierce independence, an intolerance for dishonesty, an obsession with control, and a refusal to accept the world as it was presented to him. When belonging is questioned from the beginning, the mind turns toward creation, not as art, but as survival.

He built a world in which he would never be abandoned again.

Jobs's early years were marked by restlessness. He distrusted authority, resisted structure, and rejected the idea that institutions could define him. He sought mentors, not masters; visionaries, not teachers. His rebellion was not adolescent but existential. He had seen how identities are assigned without consent. He would not accept another assigned to him.

At Apple, Jobs found a realm where his illegitimacy became an advantage.

Outsiders see what insiders cannot.

Jobs questioned every assumption the industry treated as sacred: what a computer should look like, how it should behave, who should be allowed to use it. He insisted that technology should be beautiful, intuitive, and human, even when engineers told him it was impossible. Jobs responded the way illegitimate children do when confronted with limits: he ignored them.

Where others saw boundaries, he saw failures of imagination.

His perfectionism was infamous. His demands were brutal. His certainty seemed delusional until it proved inevitable. But beneath the intensity was a simple truth: Jobs did not trust the world to get things right on its own. He had lived too long with the consequences of other people's decisions. He needed to design life on his own terms. Apple became his chosen lineage, its products his descendants, its philosophy his inheritance, its culture his creation. Jobs returned to the company after being ousted, as if reclaiming a birthright he had temporarily lost.

He resurrected it with the precision of someone who understood what it felt like to be discarded, and what it took to return stronger.

The iPod, iPhone, and iPad were not just devices. They were statements. They declared that the future would be shaped by those willing to rethink the world from its foundations, not by those who inherited authority, but by those who reinvented it.

Jobs's relationships remained marked by the same fracture as his beginnings. He sought intensity, not stability. He feared boredom more than conflict. He kept people at a distance yet demanded absolute loyalty.

He was both charismatic and uncompromising, both visionary and volatile. These contradictions were not flaws; they were consequences. Illegitimacy does not leave the psyche untouched.

In later years, Jobs sought out his biological father without knowing it, meeting him in a café he frequented, unaware of their connection.

This accidental encounter reveals something essential: identity is not erased simply because society declares it inconvenient. It persists, quietly, beneath the surface of achievement.

Jobs died in 2011, leaving behind a company that outlived him, devices that reshaped global behaviour, and a mythology that transcends technology. But his legacy is more than innovation.

It is the proof that the child who begins life without a sanctioned place can build one that commands the world's attention.

Jobs did not accept the identity handed to him. He constructed a new one. He did not inherit legitimacy. He replaced it with vision. He did not wait to belong. He made belonging irrelevant.

Steve Jobs was an adopted child, an unwanted child, an outsider, and the architect of a world in which outsiders now hold the centre. He leaves behind a final, unmistakable truth:

Illegitimacy does not prevent creation.

It intensifies it. And sometimes, it changes the world.

CHAPTER 12

OPRAH WINFREY THE UNHEARD

SILENCED EARLY, AMPLIFIED HERSELF BEYOND MEASURE

Oprah Winfrey was born into a world that had already judged her. Her mother was an unmarried teenage housemaid in rural Mississippi. Her father was absent, uncertain, and uninvolved at her birth.

From the beginning, Oprah carried the combined weight of race, poverty, gender, and illegitimacy, conditions society used to define her before she could speak.

Her life began in a single-room house, without electricity or running water, raised by a grandmother who loved her fiercely but lived in a world where a Black, illegitimate girl's future was expected to be narrow: labor, obedience, silence.

Silence was the first expectation placed on her. And it is the one she broke most completely.

Oprah's childhood was a catalogue of the brutalities that follow the unprotected child. She was passed between homes, between caretakers, between adults who were themselves struggling under systems that had no place for them.

She endured abuse, sexual, emotional, generational, and learned early that shame is often a burden placed on those least responsible for carrying it.

The illegitimate child absorbs this truth young:

when the world does not protect you, you must protect yourself.

Oprah found refuge where others might not. In books. In speech.

In the quiet discovery that her voice could reach beyond her circumstances.

As a teenager, she was sent to live with her father, Vernon Winfrey, a man with strict rules and high expectations. For many illegitimate or abandoned children, structure can feel like confinement.

For Oprah, it was relief, a signal that someone believed she was worth guiding.

But even in guidance, she felt the fracture: a father who raised her but was not her origin; a mother who birthed her but could not protect her; a society that punished her for the consequences of others' decisions.

Her ascent began not with talent but with defiance.

A refusal to disappear. A refusal to remain silent.

A refusal to accept that her story must be shaped by her beginnings.

Oprah started in local radio, then local television, her raw emotional honesty considered unprofessional at first.

She did not sound like the voices America was accustomed to hearing. She was not polished, detached, or sanitised. She was present. She was vulnerable. She was real.

The industry tried to push her into silence again, this time not about her trauma, but about her emotional instinct. News anchors were supposed to be neutral. Women were supposed to be contained. Black women, especially, were expected to be grateful for any visibility at all.

Oprah refused every expectation. Her empathy became her authority. Her vulnerability became her power. Her emotional transparency became a form of truth-telling television had never seen.

The Oprah Winfrey Show did not simply succeed. It redefined the emotional vocabulary of public life. She created a space where people could name what had been unspeakable: abuse, shame, illegitimacy, abandonment, identity, secrecy.

Her interviews were not performances; they were excavations. She did not entertain guests, she disarmed them. And she did so because she understood, more deeply than they did, what it meant to carry a story that the world wants hidden.

Oprah used her illegitimacy the way others used their lineage.

As foundation. As permission. As power.

She built an empire, not inherited, not granted, not handed down.

An empire of influence, emotion, and cultural authority.

A space where millions of people who had lived in silence found recognition.

When she spoke publicly about her childhood abuse, it was not confession. It was reclamation.

Legitimacy demands silence about shame.

Illegitimacy destroys silence by naming it.

Her philanthropy, her media network, her global influence all grew from the same impulse: to give others what she was denied. Not protection. Not pity.

A voice.

A voice strong enough to confront the sentence society once placed on her.

Oprah Winfrey is not remembered as an illegitimate child.

She is remembered as the woman who made truth a form of power.

Her origin was a mark meant to diminish her. Her life turned it into a platform. She did not inherit legitimacy.

She built credibility. She did not inherit a name.

She made her own unforgettable.

She did not inherit a place. She created a space large enough for millions.

Oprah's legacy is not entertainment.

It is disruption, the quiet, relentless dismantling of the idea that the circumstances of a child's birth determine the limits of their voice.

She was born into silence. She ended her life speaking for the world. And in her story lies one of the core truths of this book:

Illegitimacy does not erase potential. It reveals it. And sometimes, it reveals a voice powerful enough to transform a culture built on silence.

OPRAH
SHOW

SUMMARY PART IV

WHAT THE BASTARD OWE

What the bastard owes is not obedience, but clarity

Part IV turns to the modern world, where the word *bastard* is no longer written into law or stamped into baptismal records, yet its logic persists in quieter, more intimate forms.

Illegitimacy has evolved from a legal category into a psychological condition, abandonment, adoption, fatherlessness, secrecy, displacement, and the inheritance of silence. The mechanism remains the same: a child learns early that their place is negotiable, conditional, or undeserved. What changes is how they respond.

This part shows that the illegitimate child of the modern era no longer merely endures the sentence; they reinterpret it. They turn fracture into force. They transform origin into perspective. They build worlds rather than inherit them. And in doing so, they reveal what illegitimacy actually produces in the human mind: not shame, but clarity.

Charlie Chaplin, born to an unwed mother and an absent father, raised in London workhouses, emerged from the margins as the most recognisable face of the silent film era. The Tramp, his global icon, is the embodiment of illegitimacy: wandering, rootless, dignified in poverty, defiant in exclusion. Chaplin's genius grew from the sensitivity of someone who had learned as a child to read danger, emotion, and hypocrisy in an instant. His work gave a voice to those the world refused to see.

Steve Jobs began life relinquished by unmarried parents, claimed by strangers, suspended between two origins. Adoption reshaped his identity into one of fracture and reinvention, a mind relentlessly driven to impose order on chaos, to design new worlds when the existing ones felt insufficient. Jobs did not inherit his name, his culture, or his legacy; he built them all. His illegitimacy sharpened his intolerance for mediocrity and his audacious belief that the world should be redesigned from scratch.

Oprah Winfrey, born to an unwed teenage mother, raised in rural poverty, shuffled between homes, and silenced by abuse, became the opposite of what the sentence prescribed. She cracked open her own shame in public and, in doing so, dismantled the shame of millions. Her voice, emotional, raw, truth-seeking, became an authority more powerful than any inherited legitimacy. Oprah did not escape her origins; she confronted them until they became her platform.

Together, these figures show that the modern illegitimate child does not remain defined by what they were denied. Instead, they interrogate the very systems that denied them.

They do not ask for legitimacy; they expose its artificiality. They do not inherit power; they remake it.

Their lives reveal a final truth that this book has traced across centuries:

the failure of the sentence is not historical, it is ongoing.

Legitimacy cannot predict who will shape the world.

Birth cannot dictate destiny. Shame cannot silence the mind that refuses to accept it.

In the modern era, the illegitimate child owes nothing to the structures that tried to diminish them, except the clarity to see through them, and the courage to build in their ruins.

CHAPTER 13

JESUS THE ULTIMATE ILLEGITIMATE

LEGITIMATE IN HEAVEN. ILLEGITIMATE ON EARTH. UNAVOIDABLE IN HISTORY

Jesus of Nazareth entered the world under conditions that society did not easily explain.

Christian theology affirms him as the Son of God, born of the Virgin Mary — fully legitimate in a sense that transcends human categories. But this chapter concerns not his divine identity, which is unquestioned within faith, but the human social position into which he was born.

In first-century Judea, legitimacy was not symbolic. It was legal. It determined inheritance, status, religious standing, and protection. A child's place in the community came from the publicly acknowledged father. Without that recognition, a child lived outside the guarantees that shaped ordinary identity.

Jesus was born into a world ruled by that system. And within that system, he carried the marks of irregularity.

Mary conceived him before her marriage to Joseph.

Joseph was not his biological father. The explanation, divine conception, was not a category the law possessed. To the faithful, this is miracle.

To the community around them, it was mystery. In a culture without room for mystery, it was suspicion. The Gospels themselves preserve the tension. In John, Jesus's opponents say:

> *"We are not illegitimate children."*
>
> — *(JOHN 8:41)*

A remark not directed at themselves, but at him. In Mark, villagers refer to him not as

> *"the son of Joseph," but "the son of Mary."*
>
> — *(MARK 6:3)*

A small phrase with a sharp edge. Jewish men were identified by their fathers. To name him by his mother was to imply uncertainty. None of this touches theology. It describes the human environment into which theology entered. Joseph's quiet intention to "put Mary away" tells the rest.

He understood the situation's danger, for her, for the unborn child, for the fragile standing of both. His later acceptance protected Mary, but it could not erase what others assumed they saw.

Thus Jesus grew up not only in poverty and obscurity, but under a shadow of social irregularity, the kind that did not vanish simply because it was unjustified. The divine truth of his identity did not cancel the human truth of how people in his village might have spoken about him. Illegitimacy, as this book has shown, is not a fact. It is an accusation.

It is carried in whispers, in the absence of a name, in the silence of records that say less than they mean. It is defined by those who enforce it, not those who bear it.

Jesus's ministry reflects a man familiar with that condition.

He identified repeatedly with:

- the outcast
- the unclean
- the uncounted
- the children without status
- the women without witnesses
- the men without lineage
- the families without legitimacy

He spoke to them not from above, but alongside. He touched the excluded before he preached to the included. His authority, unlike that of priests, scribes, or rulers, came neither from lineage nor institution. He possessed no inherited place in the hierarchy of his time.

His legitimacy came instead from recognition: the crowds that gathered, the sick who trusted him, the disciples who followed him without contract or guarantee.

Where others taught from inheritance, he taught from presence. Where others enforced the law, he interpreted its heart. Where others guarded status, he dissolved it. His teachings on fathers and sons, earthly and divine, gain weight in this light.

A man raised under suspicion becomes the one who redefines fatherhood itself:

> *"Call no man on earth your father; for one is your Father, who is in heaven."*
>
> — *(MATTHEW 23:9)*

Not a dismissal of earthly parents. A reordering of legitimacy.

Jesus repeatedly inverted the system that measures human value through lineage. He replaced inherited status with chosen belonging. He replaced purity with mercy. He replaced the boundary with the invitation.

His life challenges every premise upon which illegitimacy depends. By the standards of his society, he lacked what mattered most: a sanctioned beginning.

By the standards of history, he built what matters more: a world in which beginnings do not determine endings.

His death, public, political, and humiliating, was the final expression of a life lived without institutional protection.

Rome found his influence destabilising; religious authorities found his disregard for inherited legitimacy intolerable. Those born outside systems often threaten the systems most.

Yet his resurrection, the cornerstone of Christian faith, redefines legitimacy entirely. What society questioned, God affirmed. What humanity disputed, eternity sealed.

This chapter is not an argument about theology. It is an argument about society. The world that questioned the circumstances of his birth was not the world he answered to.

The system that defined legitimacy could not contain the life he lived, or the legacy that followed.

If this book began with ***William the Bastard***, it ends with ***Jesus the Unfathered*** not as an equal comparison, but as a final demonstration of the truth that threads through every chapter:

Legitimacy is human. Purpose is not.

History often crowns the illegitimate. Faith goes further.o

It redeems them. And in the life of Jesus, the illegitimate child becomes the foundation of a story that outlived every system meant to define him.

REFLECTIONS

THE FAILURE OF THE SENTENCE

Illegitimacy was created to control inheritance, to protect lineage, to preserve the illusion that worth could be measured by the circumstances of birth. It was never a moral system. It was an administrative one. A bureaucratic shorthand that hardened into hierarchy, then into insult, then into shame.

The word ***bastard*** survived because it served a purpose.

Not for children, for adults.

Not for families, for institutions.

Not for order, for power.

Yet every history in this book reveals the same truth: ***the sentence failed.***

It failed because people refused to obey it.

It failed because life does not bend to the rules of those who fear disruption.

It failed because the world cannot be neatly inherited; it must constantly be rebuilt.

The kings without crowns, the creators without permission, the women without protection, the modern children of silence, all of them demonstrate that legitimacy is not the predictor society insists it is. Power does not reliably pass through sanctioned bloodlines. Genius does not respond to paperwork. Resilience does not belong to the protected.

Illegitimacy tried to decide what someone was allowed to become. History proved the arrogance of that attempt.

The individuals in these pages were not merely exceptions; they were indictments. Their lives expose the emptiness of legitimacy as a moral category. The legitimacy system, marriage, birth, inheritance, reputation, could not contain them. It could not predict them. It could not stop them.

The sentence failed because they refused the logic behind it.

And what is that logic? That a child's value is determined before they can speak. That identity is a matter of paperwork.

That dignity is something granted from above.

Every person in this book understood, consciously or instinctively, that these assumptions are false. Marginalisation sharpened them. Exclusion revealed the machinery of the world. Shame did not break them; it clarified them.

Illegitimate children often grow up reading systems with forensic precision. They learn early what is withheld, what is conditional, what is performative. They learn where power hides. They learn how protection is rationed. They see, without sentiment, how legitimacy is assigned to maintain structures, not truth.

And because they see it, they know how to move outside it.

This clarity is their inheritance, the only one society ever offered them. And they used it. They used it to create, to lead, to disrupt, to build.

The sentence failed because the world changed more through

the work of the illegitimate than through the descendants of sanctioned bloodlines.

Look at the pattern:

- A bastard conquered England.
- A bastard queen reshaped an empire.
- A hidden son ended a century-long conflict.
- Illegitimate minds invented the modern imagination, the modern economy, the modern nation, the modern technological world.
- An illegitimate girl from Mississippi became the voice of millions.
- An unwanted baby revolutionized personal technology.
- An abandoned child became the most recognized face in cinema.

These are not accidents. They are evidence. Evidence that legitimacy has nothing to do with ability.

Evidence that hierarchy is an illusion maintained by those who benefit from it.

Evidence that exclusion often produces clarity, not weakness.

Evidence that the story society tries to impose on the illegitimate child is smaller than the story that child can write for themselves.

The sentence failed because it depended on silence.

Because it depended on shame.

Because it depended on the belief that people accept the roles assigned to them. But the figures in this book did not accept those roles. They stepped outside them. They expanded them. They inherited nothing and still reshaped everything. The lesson is not that illegitimacy produces greatness. The lesson is that legitimacy does not. It never did.

The world will always create people who do not fit its categories. Children born outside the lines. Children born without permissions. Children born into circumstances that do not protect them.

What this book argues, what history confirms, is that these children are not lesser. They are not broken. They are not shameful. They are not incomplete. They are simply unpredicted. And therefore, unrestricted.

The sentence failed because it was built on a false premise: that the conditions of birth determine the limits of a life.

Every life in this book proves the opposite. The illegitimate child is not evidence of disorder. They are evidence of the world's inability to control possibility.

The sentence failed. It always will. Because the world cannot contain the people it tried hardest to erase.

ARCHITECTURE of POWER

CONCLUSION

Illegitimacy is not a mistake of birth.

It is a structure built by those who believe they have the right to decide who belongs.

Across this book, twelve lives have shown the same pattern:

- when legitimacy is withheld, identity must be constructed;
- when inheritance is denied, power must be invented;
- when protection is absent, the mind grows sharper where it is forced to stand alone

Kings, artists, soldiers, actresses, inventors, icons, each began with the same condition: a world that did not make room for them.

They did not overcome illegitimacy. They exposed it.

They revealed that legitimacy is a human invention, a boundary drawn to protect the comfortable and discipline the inconvenient. These figures lived in the space outside that boundary and proved that the space outside it is often where the future begins.

Some conquered. Some created. Some endured.

Some survived long enough to be mythologised.

But all of them lived without the assurance that the world would recognise their worth.

This book began as a study of exclusion. It ends as something else: a challenge.

A challenge to the systems that label children before they speak.

To the societies that punish those born without sanctioned origins.

To the quiet cruelties performed under the guise of morality, order, and inheritance.

And the decision to include Jesus Christ at the end of this book was not made lightly.

It was made because if society insists on using the word bastard to wound, then it must confront the truth that even the figure it reveres, prays to, and seeks moral guidance from was born into a social category the world would have treated as illegitimate.

Not spiritually. Not theologically. But socially, by the same standards that would condemn any other child born without explanation.

If that makes you uncomfortable, it should. Because the point is not to diminish him.

The point is to reveal something about us. If you cannot say the word with contempt once you realise who it would include, then you should not use it against any child at all.

Let the reader carry this forward: the next time you are tempted to judge someone by the circumstances of their birth, remember the lives in this book, the kings without crowns, the minds without permission, the women without protection, the modern bastards who built worlds from absence.

Remember that legitimacy is a comfort of the fortunate, not a measure of worth.

Remember that greatness rarely asks permission first. And remember, finally, that if history teaches anything, it is this: the bastard does not need your approval.

But your humanity demands your kindness.

The sentence ends here, not because the world has changed, but because now you know better. And that knowledge is its own form of freedom.

EPILOGUE

This book ends where your life began: with a moment you did not choose, a story you did not write, a circumstance others tried to turn into your destiny.

You arrived into a world that made decisions about you long before you could speak.

Judgments whispered in rooms you were not allowed to enter. Opinions formed before you had a chance to exist.

Silence used as a boundary. Shame handed to you like an inheritance. You were not meant to belong. Not because you lacked value, but because your existence exposed something the world did not want to admit:

That life is bigger than permission. That birth does not obey rules. That lineage is an illusion invented to comfort the powerful.

You, the illegitimate child, were the proof. And yes, this is about you, the reader. But it is also about me. The one writing these words.

The one who grew up learning exactly how sharp silence can be. The one who was branded before I knew what the word meant. The one who carried the sentence long after the world stopped speaking it aloud.

This book is my offering to you, and my apology to the child I once was, the child I did not protect, the child who learned too early that love and legitimacy were separate things.

You survived things that should have broken you. Not through strength, through necessity. Not through heroism, through instinct. Not through privilege, through clarity.

You learned to read rooms before you could read words. You learned to anticipate abandonment. You learned to shrink, to soften, to disappear, to endure.

Those were not flaws. They were preparations.

Illegitimate children grow with a radar tuned to life's most subtle dangers. We see the architecture of the world because we were never allowed to take it for granted.

We understand power because we lived without it. We understand permission because it was never given to us freely. These are not wounds. They are weapons made from experience. If you, like me, have ever felt unclaimed, remember this:

- You were never meant to be owned.
- You are not a possession.
- You are not a mistake.
- You are not an inconvenience dressed up as morality.

If you have ever felt unwanted, remember:

- You are still here.
- Someone, somewhere, chose this outcome.
- Chose *you.*
- Chose consequence over conformity.
- Chose birth over erasure.
- If you have ever felt like an accident, remember:
- Accidents spark revolutions.

- Accidents open futures.
- Accidents rewrite history.
- Your existence is not the failure of a plan.
- It is the beginning of one.

To the reader, and to the self inside this writing, hear this clearly:

- You owe nothing to the shame that was handed to you.
- You owe nothing to the silence that protected others at your expense.
- You owe nothing to the structures that determined your worth before you were allowed to define it.
- The only debt you carry is to yourself.
- To live without apology.
- To take up the space you were told you didn't deserve.
- To release the stories that were never yours to hold.
- To refuse to replicate the cruelty that shaped you.
- To build a life that does not bow to anyone's permission.

This book is about history, but it is also about healing.

It is a record of others, but it is also a letter to the child I once was , the one who still lives quietly inside me, the one who needed these words long before I knew how to write them.

You were not meant to belong. And yet, impossibly, undeniably, you do.

Not because the world made room, but because you did.

And that is enough to begin again and again .

AN OPEN LETTER TO OPRAH WINFREY

Dear Miss Winfrey,

I have wanted to write this letter my entire life, though I did not know it until this book was finished. I grew up watching you not just as a host on a screen, but as proof that someone with a beginning like mine could still create a life of meaning. Long before I understood what illegitimacy was, I recognised in you a kind of courage that felt familiar, the quiet, private courage of a child who was not protected.

As I grew older, I began to see the shape of what we shared.

You were born illegitimate.

So was I.

You never used that word, because the world made it too cruel to speak aloud. But I felt it, in the pauses, in the silences around your early years, in the way you told the truth without apologising for the circumstances of your existence.

I recognised the terrain because I had walked it too.

I will never stand on the scale of the platform you built, and I do not pretend to. But in my small way, I wrote this book around you, around the fact that the most influential woman of our time began life in the same shadow I did.

You are the living proof of the central truth of this book:

illegitimacy does not diminish a child. It diminishes the society that shames them.

You and I know the truth that polite culture rarely acknowledges:

Illegitimacy does not shape character.

It shapes survival.

It forces a child to grow sharper, faster, quieter, stronger.

It forces clarity in places where others get inheritance instead.

You and I were born into poverty.

We were born into difficulty.

We were born into girlhood without protection.

And then, on top of that, we were born illegitimate, a sentence assigned before we could speak.

You once said that "turning wounds into wisdom" was the work of your life. I believe illegitimacy is one of the oldest wounds a child can carry, a wound made not by God, but by culture. A wound created by adults but carried by children.

And you, Miss Winfrey, turned that wound into the most extraordinary wisdom.

You lifted millions with the very voice that was once silenced.

You built a platform from circumstances that were meant to limit you.

You created belonging for people who had none.

You made a life so expansive that the world had to expand with you.

That is why I am writing to you now.

Not as a fan.

Not as someone seeking endorsement.

But as a fellow bastard, reclaiming the word, refusing the shame, and hoping to change how the next generation is treated.

Modern society has created new forms of illegitimacy: not in law, but in expectation. Not in names, but in judgment.

Children are still being marked by the circumstances of their parents' choices.

Children are still inheriting shame that is not theirs.

And we both know what that shame does.

It narrows lives.

It restricts choices.

It causes gifted children to shrink themselves before the world can shrink them first.

I am writing to ask, gently, sincerely, if you would consider placing your voice beside mine, and beside the voices of every child who began life with a name the world used to wound.

Your voice changes things. It always has.

When you name a truth, the world becomes braver.

I am asking you to help name this one:

Illegitimate children deserve dignity, protection, and possibility, not punishment.

Our lives were already hard.

They did not need to be made harder by shame.

If society would dare have called even Jesus socially illegitimate, the very figure people revere and pray to, then no child, not one, should ever be made to feel lesser for the circumstances of their birth.

Miss Winfrey, I wrote this book because children like us grow up believing their beginnings define them. I wrote this book because they deserve a different story than the one we inherited. And I wrote this letter because you, more than anyone, understand what it means to turn an origin into a calling.

If you ever see this letter, know that it was written with reverence, with solidarity, and with the deep hope that the next generation of children born like us will not have to heal from the same wounds.

With gratitude, with courage, and with a shared beginning,

Caterina Mondragon

ACKNOWLEDGMENTS

I acknowledge the energy that threw me into this life, not gently, not neatly, but with force.

Light and love still found me, even when the world did not.

I was born unplanned, unwelcome, and without a place, but I carved one.

Where there was no path, I walked anyway.

Where there was no permission, I continued.

I honour my ancestors, every wound and every whisper, and yes, even my father and his family, whose refusal to unite with my mother set the stage for poverty, hardship, and exclusion.

Their rejection built the fire I stand in now.

A soft beginning might have spared the pain, but it would not have forged the steel.

I acknowledge the society that judged what it never understood, that looked away instead of offering shelter.

Its indifference shaped me, too.

I am grateful for every harsh lesson, because each one sharpened my edge.

I have built a life from ruins and silence, and I will continue to build, louder, clearer, stronger.

I reclaim the name *bastard* without apology.

I reclaim it for myself, for those who came before me, and for those who will rise after me.

To all the bastards, past, present, and still to come, the unclaimed, the unnamed, the unwanted:

You are not accidents. You are architecture. Your existence is resistance.

Your strength is your inheritance.

This book is for you.

www.ingramcontent.com/pod-product-compliance
Lightning Source LLC
LaVergne TN
LVHW091003080826
845145LV00003B/1113

* 9 7 8 1 9 1 9 4 9 1 9 1 2 *